# THE
# *Little Book of*
# NOVA
# SCOTIA

## LEN WAGG

# NIMBUS
## PUBLISHING LTD
### nimbus.ca

## *Dedication*

*For my family: Sandy, Brett, Kiya, and Jodi, who know that a drive in the
country means waiting hours for the light to be just right.*

Nimbus Publishing Limited
3731 Mackintosh St, Halifax, NS B3K 5A5
(902) 455-4286 nimbus.ca

Printed and bound in China
NB1187

Cover caption: (front cover) The Cape d'Or lighthouse on the Bay of Fundy, near Advocate Harbour. The lighthouse was rebuilt in 1965 and is now a cozy bed and breakfast.
(Back cover) Lupins grow wild in a field in Lower Economy, Nova Scotia. The spring flower can be found all around the province and is a sign that summer is here.
Library and Archives Canada Cataloguing in Publication

Wagg, Len
[Nova Scotia]
The little book of Nova Scotia / Len Wagg.

Originally published under title: Nova Scotia.
ISBN 978-1-77108-293-8 (bound)
1. Nova Scotia—Pictorial works.  I. Title.
FC2312.W325 2015     971.6'050222     C2014-907796-3

Nimbus Publishing acknowledges the financial support for its publishing activities from the Government of Canada through the Canada Book Fund (CBF) and the Canada Council for the Arts, and from the Province of Nova Scotia through Film & Creative Industries Nova Scotia. We are pleased to work in partnership with Film & Creative Industries Nova Scotia to develop and promote our creative industries for the benefit of all Nova Scotians.

# *Introduction*

ON DIGBY NECK, THE BOAR'S HEAD LIGHTHOUSE GUIDES SHIPS through the gap in the rising basalt cliffs. Cameras around my neck, I attempt to photograph it as the sun sets, my feet planted firmly on the Joe Casey Ferry, which travels between Tiverton and East Ferry. As I casually snap away, one of the crewmen comes up behind me and suggests I climb the ladder on the dock if I want to get a really good picture. "We'll wait," he says. With that, I scamper up the ladder and frame the lighthouse—a much better shot.

On my return, after the gate goes up and the ferry starts to make the short trip across the water, I am invited into the cabin. A crewman finds a piece of paper and draws a series of lines representing dirt roads, left and right turns, and finally a gated field. "People always stop here and look but the locals know the best spot. Drive across the field through the high grass and you will see a dirt track on the other side. Follow that to the trees and you will find the best view for taking pictures," he tells me.

I thank him and head east, mindful of the sun quickly setting. The bouncing headlights of the car light the bugs in the field. As I come to the spot the crewman told me about, the last hues of light are fading and I look out to see the silhouette of a huge fish weir just out from the crescent beach. The water of the incoming tide is gently darkening the sand beach. It's too dark to get a good picture, but I sit and enjoy the canvas of light and dark before me. As the crewman said, it truly is an incredible view.

In my quest to take the perfect photograph, stories like this are not unique. It seems that people in every part of the province have their own little pieces of heaven where they can go and appreciate the beauty of what we call home. It is little wonder that so many different cultures settled in Nova Scotia, beginning first with the Mi'kmaq thousands of years ago.

While the population of Nova Scotia ebbs and flows, there is still something constant about the province. Small communities celebrate their heritage with festivals, some attracting a few hundred people, some attracting tens of thousands. You can drive through small towns and see people gathered in small groups, discussing the latest news. You can stop at a local coffee shop with a kayak strapped to your roof and strike up a conversation with someone twice your age about the area's best paddling spots.

Once, when I was lost on a dirt road, I stopped at 11:00 PM and knocked on a door for directions. An older woman answered the door and told me to come in. Not wanting to make her feel uncomfortable so late at night, I told her I was fine outside but just needed directions. She quickly shooed me in, claiming the flies would "eat me alive," and before I knew it, I was sitting at the table with a cup of tea in front of me.

That's the way it is in Nova Scotia: people help each other without a second thought. During the famine in Ethiopia in the early 1980s, Nova Scotians donated the most per capita of any Canadian province to the relief effort. The province seems to host an incredible number of charity walks and runs. In Halifax, for example, thousands of people participate in the "Run for the Cure" to end breast cancer every year.

This helping attitude and friendly way seems ingrained in who we are. Does it come from our unique combination of cultural roots? Or is it the geography of the land?

You can't help but feel small when you see the sun rise over the red cliffs of Cape Blomidon, the mist filling the valleys of the Cape Breton Highlands, or the warm light of a winter sunrise bathing Halifax Harbour. When you stand and watch the waves pound the Peggy's Cove granite, as they have for thousands of years, you understand that our tenure here is a short one. While we build houses and roads and try to shape the land, it's easy to understand that in the end, it is the land that shapes us.

**ABOVE** :~ A biker makes his way down one of the many trails in Kejimkujik National Park in the southwestern part of the province. The park features backcountry campsites and an abundance of wildlife. It is also a National Historic Site, as Mi'kmaw petroglyphs can be found on the shores of Kejimkujik Lake.

**OVERLEAF** :~ A granite rock garden emerges from the Roseway River near Indian Fields, Shelburne County. The Roseway and connecting rivers flow in from the Tobeatic Wilderness Area.

**ABOVE** ∾ Rich silt deposits built up over thousands of years make for ideal farmland around Shubenacadie and its river.

**FACING** ∾ A lone paddler makes her way down the Shubenacadie Canal near Port Wallace. The canal follows a river and lake system first used by the Mi'kmaq. Canal construction began in 1826 with the hopes of using a series of locks to improve transportation into and out of Halifax. Financial and logistical problems plagued the various companies that tried to complete the project, and the canal fell into disrepair. Over the last few decades, however, several of the canal locks have been reconstructed, and parks and hiking trails now allow visitors a glimpse of the canal's past.

**OVERLEAF** ∾ Symphony of light: A lone figure stands in front of a rare display of northern lights, or aurora borealis, in the Cobequid Mountains in Cumberland County. The lights are a result of charged particles from the sun entering the earth's atmosphere.

**ABOVE** ∿ Two Sable Island horses make their way along the beach as the surf pounds against the shore. The crescent-shaped island off the south coast of Nova Scotia is just over 40 kilometres long and 1.5 kilometres at its widest point, but despite its small size, it is home to wild horses, shorebirds, and grey seals.

**FACING** ∿ A small sailboat makes its way into Peggys Cove in the eastern entrance to St. Margarets Bay. The tiny cove, one of the most photographed areas in the province, is a magnet for those inspired by crashing seas and a massive granite shoreline.

**ABOVE** :∿ *Tea-coloured water flows from the Tom Tidney over the rocks and by a mill in Shelburne County.*

**ABOVE** ∻ A historic building in Shelburne rises up against a bright blue sky. Shelburne was founded by immigrant Loyalists—Americans who remained loyal to the British Crown—in May 1783. Black slaves from south of the border also came to Nova Scotia, and these Black Loyalists founded the largest settlement of free Blacks on the continent at Birchtown, near Shelburne.

**ABOVE** ∿ With sand and salt underfoot, beachgoers at Lawrencetown Beach enjoy their day in the sun. Located on the province's Eastern Shore, Lawrencetown is an ideal spot for surfers, swimmers, and sun worshippers during the hot summer months.

**FACING** ∿ A surfer rides a wave near Lawrencetown Beach on the Eastern Shore. The quality of the beach's waves draws surfers from as far away as Australia and California.

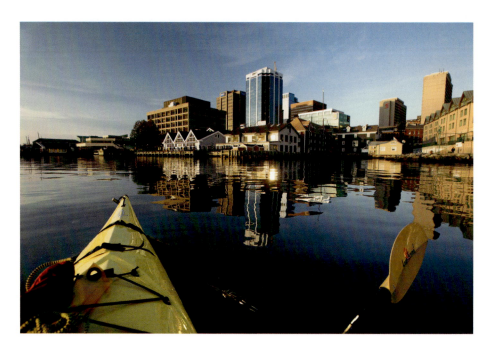

**ABOVE** ∿ The sun rises over a still Halifax Harbour. The city was founded in 1749 as a deterrent to France's Fortress in Louisbourg. It is the capital city of Nova Scotia.

**ABOVE** :~ A rainbow of colours ignites a sky already twinkling with city light. Fired from the Angus L. Macdonald Bridge deck—fifty-four metres above Halifax Harbour—the city's annual Natal Day fireworks are a crowd favourite.

**OVERLEAF** :~ The Peggys Cove light under the stars.

**RIGHT** :~ The Mersey River overflows its banks in Kejimkujik National Park. With its maze of rivers and lakes, the park is one of the province's jewels.

**ABOVE** ∿ Sailing vessels and yachts dock at the Oak Island Resort in Western Shore on the province's South Shore. Nearby Oak Island has long been thought to hold buried treasure, but despite numerous expeditions to the island, no one has yet laid claim to any prize.

**FACING** ∿ An antique car, carefully kept, sits in a barn that is a little older near Amherst, Nova Scotia.

**OVERLEAF** ∿ Wispy clouds float over the snow at the Memorial Church at the Grand Pré National Historic Site. The church was reconstructed in the same location as the original Church of Saint-Charles, where Acadians learned they were being deported in 1755.

ACADIA UNIVERSITY

FOUNDED 1838

**ABOVE** ⁓ A graduate and friend look at a photograph captured on graduation day at Acadia University in Wolfville. Established in 1838, Acadia has become one of the leading universities in the country, attracting students from around the world.

**FACING** ⁓ Playful straw people hold the Acadian flag at this farm in Ste. Anne du Ruisseau in Yarmouth County. Ste. Anne du Ruisseau is located along the Lighthouse Route just north of Pubnico, the oldest Acadian village in the province.

**ABOVE** :~ The International Space Station leaves a streak of light, and stars blur in the long exposure as it soars over the Bay of Fundy in Greenhill, Nova Scotia.

**FACING** :~ The Thinkers' Lodge in Pugwash, the former summer home of Canadian-born businessman and philanthropist Cyrus Eaton. In 1957, Eaton invited some of the world's top scientists to Pugwash for talks aimed at avoiding nuclear conflict. It was the first so-called Pugwash Conference, and the organization formed afterward was awarded the Nobel Peace Prize in 1995 for its role in helping to reduce armed conflict. In 2008, the Thinkers' Lodge (as Eaton's home is now known) was designated a place of national historic significance.

**OVERLEAF** :~ Though empty in this photo, Melmerby Beach Provincial Park is a popular spot for seals in the middle of winter. Coming across the thin ice of the Northumberland Strait, female seals land on the shore to bear their pups.

**ABOVE** :~ The tiny community of Meat Cove at the northern tip of Cape Breton Island. Meat Cove provides a perfect starting point for campers and hikers who want to visit Polletts Cove.

**FACING** :~ A mother Hereford looks warily over her brood as they make their way across a field near Mabou, Cape Breton.

**ABOVE** ⌇ Surrounded by a sun dog, or sun halo, an Air Canada jet lands at Halifax Robert L. Stanfield International Airport. Sun halos happen when light is bent by ice crystals high in the atmosphere, and are nature's way of indicating a change in the weather.

**FACING** ⌇ This columnar basalt sea stack rises into the air on the shore of St. Mary's Bay on Long Island, Digby County. Though the rocks around it have been eroded by the tides and waves, this one has found a precarious balance.

**ABOVE** ᛌ The *Carnival Victory* cruise ship dwarfs Georges Island in Halifax Harbour as it prepares to leave. The province's cruise ship industry has seen tremendous growth over the past few years as more and more tourists take to the sea.

**ABOVE** :~ The *Bluenose II* leaves Halifax Harbour on a morning cruise, proving that sometimes history does repeat itself. Launched in 1963 and modelled after the famous racing schooner *Bluenose*, the *Bluenose II* shares many of the same shipwrights as the celebrated original.

**ABOVE** :~ Doug Creelman holds on to a team of Percheron horses that makes up half of an eight-horse hitch at the Nova Scotia Provincial Exhibition in Truro. His team competes all over North America and has won the coveted World Percheron Congress twice.

**FACING** :~ An array of horseshoes welcomes visitors to the historic blacksmith shop in Sherbrooke.

**ABOVE** ~ The entrance to the Habitation at Port Royal. A National Historic Site today, Port Royal was established in 1605 by the French and is the site of the first permanent European settlement in North America.

**FACING** ~ Bait barrels sit stacked against a fishing shanty in Yarmouth Bar, Yarmouth County. Though advances in technology have made some changes to commercial fishing, wooden barrels like these are still used by many fishers.

**ABOVE** ∿ Fossils picked up along the beach in Joggins are left behind for another explorer to find. Joggins fossils have been dated back to the Carboniferous age, over three hundred million years ago.

**FACING** ∿ The sun goes down over the Joggins cliffs. In 2008, the coastline along the Joggins Fossil Cliffs was designated a UNESCO World National Heritage Site.

**ABOVE** ∿ A thunderstorm rolls down the Bay of Fundy near Cape Blomidon. The harvested blueberry fields above the town of Parrsboro turn red in the late fall.

**FACING** ∿ The cable ferry *Caolas Silas* makes its way across a portion of the Bras d'Or Lake system at Little Narrows in Cape Breton.

**ABOVE** :∼ Fishing boats sit moored near Delhaven, Kings County.

**FACING** :∼ Old ways and new technology provide a sharp contrast near Cheticamp. With the strong winds blowing off the Northumberland Strait, the Cape Breton Highlands are an ideal location for wind power.

**ABOVE** ∾ An old lighthouse and a crumbling dwelling are all that remain on Devils Island, near the mouth of Halifax Harbour. The island was home to several permanent residents until most were relocated to the mainland in the 1940s.

**ABOVE** ∾ Golfers at the Parrsboro Golf Club in Greenhill, Cumberland County, tee off on immaculate turf. Golfers at the nine-hole course enjoy spectacular views while trying to avoid the giant water trap referred to as the Minas Basin.

**ABOVE** :~ Shannon Ward of Parrsboro navigates her way through a blueberry field in Lakelands, Cumberland County. With its hundreds of hectares of berries picked by hand and machine, Nova Scotia is one of the largest blueberry producers in the world.

**FACING** :~ Wild blueberries, ready for picking, hang on a bush in Lakelands, Cumberland County.

**ABOVE** ∿ Frothy waves rush over the beach stones near Cape Chignecto Provincial Park. A popular destination for hikers, the park features over fifty kilometres of trails, many of which skirt the spectacular coastline.

**FACING** ∿ Canada's first National Historic Site, Fort Anne, is a reminder of the volatile times of European settlement in Canada. Fort Anne was pivotal in the ongoing battles between the French and English for control of North America. The Field Officer's Quarters, pictured here, was built in 1797 and remains one of the most recognized symbols of the town of Annapolis Royal.

**ABOVE** :~ In the choppy waves of the Minas Basin, a lobster boat motors away from the cliffs of Cape Blomidon. According to Mi'kmaw legend, the bluffs of Blomidon were home to the great Glooscap.

**ABOVE** ⁓ Tiny barnacles cling to rocks in the shadow of the Brothers Islands in the Minas Basin. The islands' old-growth forests provide a perfect nesting ground for eagles, just one of many reasons the Brothers Islands are owned and protected by the Nova Scotia Nature Trust.

**ABOVE** ∿ Two Halflinger horses check out an intruder to their pasture near Bass River.

**FACING** ∿ Horses graze near Middleton in the heart of the Annapolis Valley. The valley is one of the province's most important agricultural regions and is well-known for its apple crop.

**ABOVE** ∻ A snowboarder bites into the trail at Ski Wentworth, near Truro.

**ABOVE** :~ Winter at Victoria Park in Truro. The park's Lepper Brook, pictured here, features two sets of waterfalls.

**ABOVE** :~ Dave Alder goes airborne while sea kayaking in Lower Prospect. Located between Halifax Harbour and Peggys Cove, Lower Prospect is a popular kayaking spot with a sad history. On April 1, 1873, the SS *Atlantic* ran aground here, killing 562 passengers and crew. Thanks to the efforts of the local community, 390 passengers were rescued.

**FACING** :~ A colourful collection of sea kayaks sits on a beach in Lower Prospect. With its countless coves and inlets, and with 7,400 kilometres of coastline, Nova Scotia is a favourite destination for kayakers.

**OVERLEAF** :~ The lanterns of ice fishers illuminate the snow on Cape Breton's Nyanza Bay near the First Nations community of Wagmatcook.

**ABOVE** ∿ As the home of the *Bluenose* and *Bluenose II* (pictured at left), Lunenburg has a prominent place in Nova Scotia's seafaring past. Founded in 1753, the town has stayed true to its heritage by keeping its original colonial settlement design.

**ABOVE** :~ One of the most recognizable sights of Nova Scotia's South Shore is the view of the three churches at Mahone Bay—St. James' Anglican, St. John's Lutheran, and Trinity United.

**ABOVE** ꞉∼ The Cape d'Or lighthouse on the Bay of Fundy, near Advocate Harbour. The lighthouse was rebuilt in 1965 and is now a cozy bed and breakfast.

**FACING** ꞉∼ A family heads toward safer ground as the incoming tide pounds the shoreline off Cape d'Or. The huge waves in this area—some of the highest in the world—are caused by the Dory Rips, the force of three tidal paths coming together at one point.

**RIGHT** ∾ A young woman takes a picture from the vantage point at Cape Clear, Cape Breton. Overlooking the Margaree Valley from the Cape Breton Highlands plateau, Cape Clear is one of the province's premier vantage points.

**ABOVE** :~ With the water on both sides, the Keltic Lodge in Ingonish offers an unparalleled view. Opened in 1940, the lodge is one of three owned by the province. With a pool, cabins, fine dining, golf, and quick access to Cape Breton Highlands National Park, the lodge is a preferred stopping point for visitors to Cape Breton.

**ABOVE** ∻ Deep river valleys, an old-growth forest, and spectacular coastline all make the Cabot Trail one of the most scenic roadways in the world. This view is of the Gulf of St. Lawrence near Pleasant Bay.

**OVERLEAF** ∻ The moon sets behind Saint Margaret of Scotland Church on the River Denys Mountain in Cape Breton. Though the church is all that is left of a once-thriving community, a service is still held here each year.

**ABOVE** ∿ An idle tractor in a hayfield, near Blomidon. For hundreds of years the lands around the Minas Basin have provided rich soil for agriculture.

**ABOVE** ~ A gentle snow coats this farm near Antigonish. A familiar sight along the Trans-Canada Highway, farms like this one sprawl across many parts of inland Nova Scotia.

**ABOVE** ∿ A small lighthouse stands guard at sunset on Grand Eddy Point, Digby County. Only one ship—the *Pronto*—was ever wrecked on Grand Eddy Point. In February 1880, the sailing vessel left Yarmouth only to meet its end in bad weather at the point.

**ABOVE** ∿ A collection of sea glass and shells sits on a deck in the Bay of Fundy. Sea glass is a result of bottles being broken and tumbled by the action of the water and rocks.